Costa Rica Travel Guide 2023

The Ultimate Travel Guide For Planning Your Trip To Costa Rica with the Essential Information to Discover the Best of Costa Rica like a Local

Joseph Navas

Copyright 2023 by Joseph Navas - All rights reserved.

This document is geared towards providing exact and reliable information in regards to the topic and issue covered. The publication is sold with the idea that the publisher is not required to render accounting, officially permitted, or otherwise, qualified services. If advice is necessary, legal or professional, a practiced individual in the profession should be ordered.

From a Declaration of Principles which was accepted and approved equally by a Committee of the American Bar Association and a Committee of Publishers and Associations.

In no way is it legal to reproduce, duplicate, or transmit any part of this document in either electronic means or in printed format. Recording of this publication is strictly prohibited and any storage of this document is not allowed unless with written permission from the publisher. All rights reserved.

The information provided herein is stated to be truthful and consistent, in that any liability, in terms of inattention or otherwise, by any usage or abuse of any policies, processes, or directions contained within is the solitary and utter responsibility of the recipient reader. Under no circumstances will any legal responsibility or blame be held against the publisher for any reparation, damages, or monetary loss due to the information herein, either directly or indirectly.

Respective authors own all copyrights not held by the publisher.

The information herein is offered for informational purposes solely, and is universal as so. The presentation of the information is without contract or any type of guarantee assurance.

COSTA RICA TRAVEL GUIDE 2023

The trademarks that are used are without any consent, and the publication of the trademark is without permission or backing by the trademark owner. All trademarks and brands within this book are for clarifying purposes only and are the owned by the owners themselves, not affiliated with this document.

All rights reserved. No part of this book may be used or reproduced in any form whatsoever without written permission except in the case of brief quotations in critical articles or reviews.

Printed in the United States of America.

ISBN - Paperback: 978-1-80362-208-8

First Edition: Marz 2023

JOSEPH NAVAS

CONTENTS

COSTA RICA TRAVEL GUIDE 2023 1

CONTENTS 4

CHAPTER 1 1

INTRODUCTION TO THE COSTA RICA 1

CHAPTER 2 8

WHAT TO SEE IN COSTA RICA 8

CHAPTER 3 25

WHAT TO DO IN COSTA RICA ? 25

CHAPTER 4 31

WHAT TO EAT IN COST RICA? 31

CHAPTER 5 44

PRATICAL TIPS FOR TRAVELING IN COSTA RICA 44

CHAPTER 6 53

OTHER TIPS TO TRAVELING IN COSTA RICA 53

CHAPTER 7 63

SAN JOSE 63

CHAPTER 8 74

MONTE VERDE 74

CHAPTER 1

INTRODUCTION TO THE COSTA RICA

A brief history of the country

Costa Rica is a country located in the south-central part of Central America, with an area of about 51,000 km² and a population of just over 5 million. Its history dates back to before the arrival of Europeans to the American continent, when the territory was inhabited by several indigenous tribes who lived mainly from agriculture, fishing and hunting.

In 1502, Spanish navigator Christopher Columbus touched the Costa Rican coast on his fourth voyage to the Americas, but it was not until 1524 that the Spanish began colonizing the country, in search of gold and other riches. Over the next few decades, indigenous peoples were subdued and converted to Christianity, while the first cities were built, including Cartago, the country's first capital.

During the colonial period, Costa Rica was included in the viceroyalty of Peru, but it retained some administrative autonomy due to its remoteness from the main Spanish cities and lack of natural resources that could attract the attention of invaders. However, Spanish colonization had a significant impact on Costa Rican culture and society, bringing new languages, religions and traditions.

In 1821, Costa Rica gained independence from Spain along with other Spanish colonies in Central America, forming the United Provinces of Central America. In 1838, the United Provinces dissolved and Costa Rica became a fully independent state. During the 19th century, the country experienced a period of political instability, marked by a series of civil wars and conflicts with neighboring countries, such as Nicaragua.

In the 20th century, Costa Rica experienced a phase of modernization and economic development, thanks to the opening of new production sectors, such as coffee and bananas, and the construction of road and port infrastructure. In 1948, the country experienced an event that changed its history: a brief but violent civil war that led to the fall of the incumbent president and the creation of a new constitution, which abolished the army and promoted democracy and human rights.

Since then, Costa Rica has become a model of political stability and sustainable development, thanks to its focus on environmental protection and the well-being of its inhabitants. Tourism is a major sector of the Costa Rican economy, thanks to its outstanding natural beauty, with national parks, beaches, rainforests, and active volcanoes, as well as its vibrant culture and friendly, welcoming people.

In recent years, Costa Rica has faced some challenges, such as the growth of crime.

General information on climate, geography, and culture

Costa Rica is a country located in the south-central part of Central America, between Nicaragua to the north and Panama to the south. With an area of about 51,000 km², Costa Rica is one of the smallest nations on the American continent, but it is also one of the richest in biodiversity and natural beauty.

Costa Rica's climate is tropical and humid, with two main seasons: the dry season, which runs from December to May, and the rainy season, which runs from June to November. However, the climate varies greatly by region and altitude: coastal areas are hot and humid year-round, with average temperatures around 30°C, while mountain areas are cooler and drier, with temperatures that can drop as low as 10°C at night.

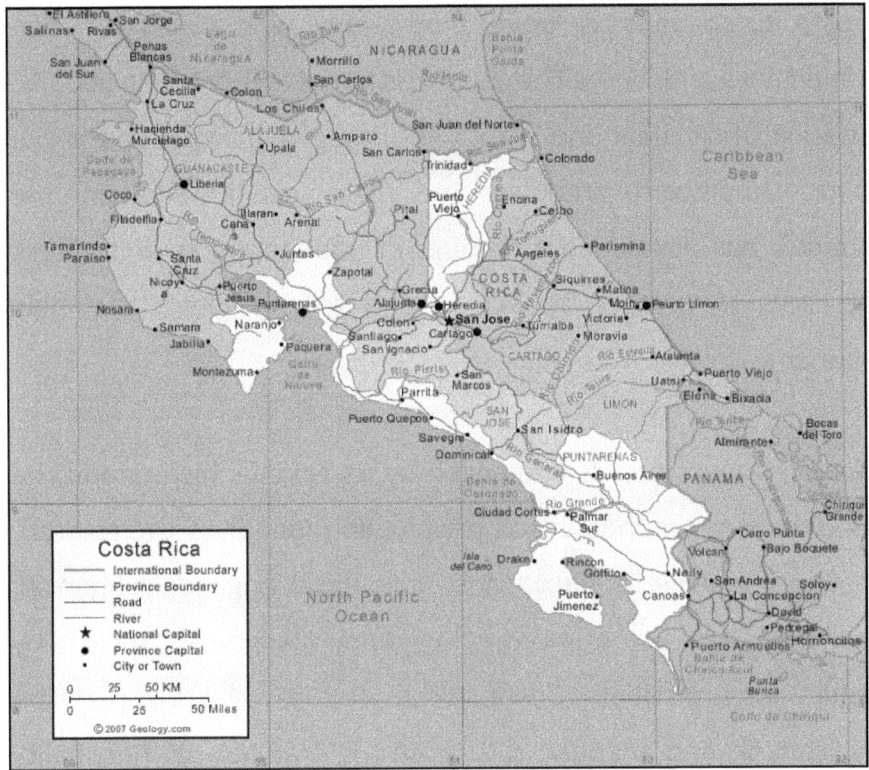

Questa foto di Autore sconosciuto è concesso in licenza da CC BY-NC

Costa Rica's geography is very diverse, with three mountain ranges crossing the country from north to south and several coastal plains. The largest mountain range is the Cordillera de Talamanca, which stretches along the border with Panama and is home to the country's highest point, Cerro Chirripó, which reaches 3,820 meters (10,000 feet) in elevation. Other important mountain ranges are the Cordillera de Guanacaste, in the northwest of the country, and the Cordillera Central, which crosses the country from north to south.

COSTA RICA TRAVEL GUIDE 2023

Costa Rica is famous for its biodiversity, with a very rich and varied flora and fauna. The country is home to more than 500,000 species of animals and plants, including numerous species of birds, amphibians, reptiles, and mammals. In addition, the country has developed a number of national parks and nature reserves to protect its wildlife and to promote sustainable tourism.

Costa Rica's culture is influenced by its colonial history and the traditions of the indigenous people who inhabited the territory before the arrival of Europeans. The official language is Spanish, but there are also numerous indigenous languages spoken by native communities. Costa Rican culture is known to be welcoming and friendly, with a strong tradition of hospitality toward tourists and foreigners.

Music and dance are important in Costa Rican culture, with a variety of musical genres and traditional dances, such as merengue, cumbia, and salsa. Costa Rica is also famous for its high-quality coffee, which is one of the country's main exports.

The prevailing religion in Costa Rica is Christianity, with the majority of the population following the Roman Catholic Church. However, there are also numerous other religions present in the country, including Protestantism, Islam, and Buddhism.

CHAPTER 2

WHAT TO SEE IN COSTA RICA

Major cities and places of tourist interest

Costa Rica offers many places of tourist interest, both for nature lovers and for those seeking art and culture. Listed below are some of the main cities and tourist attractions in Costa Rica:

- San José: The country's capital is a modern and vibrant city with numerous museums, restaurants, and stores. Highlights include the National Theater, the Metropolitan Cathedral, and the National Museum.

- Puerto Viejo de Talamanca: This resort on the Caribbean coast is famous for its white sand beaches and relaxed atmosphere. Surfing, snorkeling and scuba diving can be enjoyed here, as well as Caribbean cuisine.

- Monteverde: Located in the northern mountains of the country, Monteverde is an ideal destination for nature lovers and birdwatchers. It is home to the Monteverde Biological Reserve, which is home to numerous hiking trails and a wide variety of plant and animal species.

- Tortuguero National Park: This park on the Caribbean coast is famous for its beaches where sea turtles come to lay their eggs. Other animal species such as caimans, iguanas and pumas can also be seen here.

Questa foto di Autore sconosciuto è concesso in licenza da CC BY

- Arenal: This location in the northwest of the country is famous for the Arenal volcano, which was still active until 2010. Here you can hike in the mountains, enjoy the hot springs, and visit the La Fortuna waterfall.

- Manuel Antonio: Located on the Pacific coast, Manuel Antonio is one of Costa Rica's most popular beach resorts, with white sandy beaches and a wide variety of flora and fauna. Manuel Antonio National Park is located here and is home to numerous animal species, including monkeys, iguanas, and toucans.

- Guanacaste: this province located in the northwestern part of the country offers many tourist attractions, including Rincon de la Vieja National Park, Tamarindo beaches, and traditional Costa Rican haciendas.

- Corcovado: Located on the Pacific coast in the southern part of the country, Corcovado National Park is one of Costa Rica's most beautiful and pristine natural areas, with a wide variety of plant and animal species.

These are just a few of the tourist attractions in Costa Rica, which offers numerous other attractions for visitors of all types.

National Parks and Nature Reserves on the Costa Rica

Costa Rica is famous for its biodiversity and its commitment to environmental conservation. For this reason, the country is home to numerous nature reserves and national parks that have become destinations for tourists from all over the world. Some of Costa Rica's most important national parks and nature reserves are listed below:

- **Tortuguero National Park:** located on the Caribbean coast, the park is famous for its wide variety of wildlife, including sea turtles, caimans, iguanas, and tropical birds. Here you can take boat trips along the canals and visit beaches where turtles lay their eggs.

- **Manuel Antonio National Park:** located on the Pacific coast, the park is famous for its white sand beaches and wildlife, including monkeys, iguanas and toucans. Here you can hike along the park's trails and enjoy the beaches.

- **Corcovado National Park:** located in the southern part of the country, the park is considered one of Costa Rica's most pristine natural areas, with a wide variety of plant and animal species. Here you can hike along the park's trails and observe wildlife.

- **Monteverde Biological Reserve:** located in the northern mountains of the country, the reserve is famous for its wide variety of bird species and vegetation. Here you can hike along the park's trails and visit the famous Monteverde suspension bridge.

- **Rincon de la Vieja National Park:** located in Guanacaste province, the park is famous for the Rincon de la Vieja volcano and its geothermal activities. Here you can hike along the park's trails and visit waterfalls and natural pools.

- **Curi-Cancha Biological Reserve:** located in the Monteverde area, the reserve is home to a wide variety of animal and plant species, including monkeys, hummingbirds, and orchids. Here you can hike along the park's trails and visit the Curicancha house museum.

- **Cahuita National Park**: located on the Caribbean coast, the park is famous for its white sand beaches and wide variety of marine life. Here you can hike along the park's trails and snorkel in the crystal clear waters.

These are just a few of Costa Rica's national parks and nature reserves, which offer many other opportunities to discover the beauty of its nature and biodiversity.

Beaches and beach resorts Costa Rica

Costa Rica is famous for its biodiversity and rainforests, but it also offers a number of beautiful beaches and beach resorts that attract tourists from all over the world. Some of Costa Rica's most popular beaches and beach resorts are listed below:

Tamarindo: Located on the Pacific coast in Guanacaste province, Tamarindo is a popular tourist destination famous for its long white sand beaches and crystal clear waters ideal for surfing and snorkeling. The town offers a lively nightlife scene with a wide selection of bars and restaurants.

Manuel Antonio: Located on the Pacific coast, Manuel Antonio is another popular vacation spot offering white sand beaches surrounded by rainforests and a wide range of activities such as surfing, snorkeling, and kayaking. Manuel Antonio National Park, located nearby, is one of the most visited national parks in Costa Rica.

Jaco: Located on the Pacific coast in the province of Puntarenas, Jaco is a popular tourist destination among surfers and nightlife enthusiasts. Here you will find beaches with waves ideal for surfing and a wide range of restaurants and bars.

Questa foto di Autore sconosciuto è concesso in licenza da CC BY-NC-ND

Questa foto di Autore sconosciuto è concesso in licenza da CC BY-SA-NC

COSTA RICA TRAVEL GUIDE 2023

Puerto Viejo: Located on the Caribbean coast in the province of Limon, Puerto Viejo is a popular tourist destination with white sandy beaches and crystal clear waters ideal for swimming and snorkeling. Some of the best seafood restaurants in Costa Rica can also be found here.

Questa foto di Autore sconosciuto è concesso in licenza da CC BY-SA

Playa Samara: Located on the Pacific coast in the province of Guanacaste, Playa Samara is a beautiful beach with calm, tranquil waters ideal for swimming and kayaking. Some of the best restaurants in the region can also be found here.

Questa foto di Autore sconosciuto è concesso in licenza da CC BY-SA-NC

Santa Teresa: located on the Pacific coast in Puntarenas province, Santa Teresa is a popular tourist destination among surfers. Here you will find beaches with waves ideal for surfing and a wide range of restaurants and bars.

These are just a few of the beautiful beaches and beach resorts Costa Rica has to offer. Each of these destinations offers a unique combination of beautiful beaches, outdoor activities, and local restaurants, making them unique and memorable.

Costa Rica is one of the havens for outdoor tourism and nature adventures. With its wide range of ecosystems and landscapes, from rainforest to mountains, Pacific and Atlantic Ocean coasts, it offers numerous opportunities for outdoor activities. Some of the most popular outdoor activities in Costa Rica are described below:

Trekking: Costa Rica offers numerous trekking opportunities through its rainforests, national parks, and nature reserves. Corcovado National Park, located on the Pacific coast, is one of the best places for trekking, with a wide range of trails leading to waterfalls, remote beaches and rainforests.

Rafting: Costa Rica is famous for its world-class rapids, which attract rafting enthusiasts from all over the world. The Pacuare River, located in Limon province, is one of the best places for rafting, with rapids ranging from class III to class IV. The Sarapiqui River, located in Heredia province, also offers excellent rafting opportunities.

Surfing: Costa Rica is known as one of the best places in the world to surf because of its perfect waves and ideal weather conditions. The Pacific coast is an ideal surfing destination, with some of the best beaches for the sport such as Tamarindo, Jaco, Dominical, and Playa Grande. The Caribbean coast also offers some surfing opportunities, particularly in Puerto Viejo.

Snorkeling: Costa Rica offers a unique snorkeling experience due to its wide range of marine life and breathtaking underwater landscapes. Cahuita Marine National Park, located on the Caribbean coast, is one of the best places for snorkeling, with a wide range of marine species including tropical fish, sea turtles, and coral. The Pacific coast also offers some snorkeling opportunities, particularly in the vicinity of Manuel Antonio National Park.

Canopy tours: The Canopy tour, also known as a zip-line tour, is an exciting experience that allows you to fly through the treetops of the rainforest. Costa Rica offers numerous opportunities for Canopy tours, including Monteverde, Arenal and La Fortuna.

Horseback Excursions: Horseback excursions are a unique experience to explore Costa Rica's nature. Through this activity, it is possible to visit some of the country's most remote and less-traveled areas, such as remote mountains and beaches. Rincon de la Vieja National Park, located in Guanacaste province, is one of the best places for horseback riding excursions.

Canyoning: Canyoning is a popular activity in Costa Rica and offers a thrilling experience through rainforest gorges. La Fortuna

Waterfall is one of the most popular places for canyoning and offers a number of waterfalls from which to take the plunge.

These are just a few of the most popular outdoor activities Costa Rica has to offer. Each of these activities offers a unique experience that allows you to explore the natural beauty of the country and experience the adrenaline rush of outdoor activities.

CHAPTER 3

WHAT TO DO IN COSTA RICA ?

Nature and wildlife exploration in Costa Rica

Costa Rica is an ideal destination for those who enjoy exploring nature and observing wildlife. Due to its geographical location, Costa Rica has a wide range of natural habitats, from rainforests to coastal wetlands, which support a unique variety of flora and fauna. Below are some nature and wildlife exploration activities that we recommend you try during your trip to Costa Rica.

Rainforest hiking: Costa Rica has some of the most spectacular rainforests in the world, and rainforest hiking is one of the most popular activities for nature lovers. Corcovado National Park, Bosque de los Niños Biological Reserve, and Bosque Nuboso Monteverde Biological Reserve are just some of the places where rainforest hiking is possible.

Bird Spotting: Costa Rica is a bird lover's paradise, with more than 800 species in the country. Some of the best destinations for bird spotting include Bosque del Rio Tigre Biological Reserve, Carara Biological Reserve, and Palo Verde National Park.

Wildlife tours: Costa Rica has a wide range of wildlife, including monkeys, toucans, jaguars, pumas, and crocodiles. Wildlife tours are an excellent opportunity to see these animals in the wild. Some of the best places for wildlife tours include Tortuguero National Park, Manuel Antonio National Park, and Bosque del Cabo Biological Reserve.

Sea turtle watching: Costa Rica is one of the best places in the world for sea turtle watching. Green and giant turtles nest on the Pacific coast and the Caribbean coast of Costa Rica. The best places for sea turtle watching include Tortuguero National Park, Ostional Nature Reserve, and Playa Grande Beach.

Waterfall visits: Costa Rica has a wide range of spectacular waterfalls, some of which can only be reached on foot or by boat. La Fortuna Falls, Rio Celeste Falls, and Montezuma Falls are just a few of the most popular waterfalls worth visiting.

Horseback riding: Horseback riding is a great activity to explore nature and see wildlife in Costa Rica. Some of the best destinations for horseback hiking include the Bosque del Cabo Biological Reserve, Rincon de la Vieja National Park, and the Arenal Volcano area.

Guided tours of coffee plantations and cocoa plantations in Costa Rica

Costa Rica is famous for producing high quality coffee and chocolate. Guided tours of coffee plantations and cocoa farms are an excellent opportunity to learn about the production of these delicious delicacies and learn more about the country's agricultural culture.

Guided tours to coffee plantations usually include a walk through the coffee fields and a detailed explanation of the coffee harvesting, processing, and roasting process. You will also taste different types of coffee and learn the secrets of a good cup of coffee. Some of Costa Rica's most famous coffee plantations include Finca Rosa Blanca, Doka Estate, and Café Britt.

Guided tours of cocoa farms, on the other hand, include a walk through cocoa fields, where visitors can see the cocoa trees and learn how they are grown. Visitors will also be able to watch the cocoa processing process and learn how it is made into chocolate. In addition, there will be tastings of artisanal chocolate and chocolates. Some of Costa Rica's most famous cocoa farms include Tirimbina Rainforest Center and La Iguana Chocolate Farm.

On both tours, participants will have the opportunity to interact with local producers and learn more about Costa Rica's farming culture. These guided tours also provide an opportunity to purchase local products and support the local economy.

In general, Costa Rica is a country that promotes sustainable agriculture and fair trade. Many of the coffee plantations and cocoa farms that offer tours adopt sustainable farming practices and pay fair wages to workers. This means that visiting these plantations and farms not only provides a unique experience, but also supports fair and sustainable trade.

Costa Rica's natural hot springs are one of the country's most popular attractions, offering visitors a relaxing and wellness experience in a spectacular natural setting. Costa Rica's thermal waters are heated by underground volcanic activity and are rich in minerals beneficial to the body, such as calcium, magnesium, and potassium.

Relaxation in the natural hot springs of the Costa Rica

There are many natural hot springs in Costa Rica, some of which have been developed into spa complexes with additional facilities and services, while others are still completely natural. Some of the most famous natural hot springs in Costa Rica include:

Tabacon Hot Springs: Located at the foot of the Arenal volcano, these natural hot springs are nestled in lush rainforest vegetation. Here you can relax in natural hot springs pools, soak in waterfalls and enjoy rejuvenating spa treatments.

Baldi Hot Springs: These natural hot springs are also located at the foot of the Arenal Volcano and offer a series of thermal pools with different temperatures and whirlpools. The hot springs complex also has restaurants, bars and activities such as a rock climbing wall.

Eco Termales Hot Springs: Located in the La Fortuna region, these natural hot springs are surrounded by lush tropical vegetation. Here you can relax in natural hot springs pools, enjoy rejuvenating massages and sample local cuisine at the on-site restaurant.

Rio Perdido: Located in the Guanacaste region, this spa complex offers a series of natural thermal pools, nature hiking trails, and activities such as tubing on the river.

La Fortuna Natural Hot Springs: Located in the La Fortuna region, these natural hot springs are completely surrounded by rainforest and offer a series of natural hot springs pools, waterfalls, and nature hiking trails.

Costa Rica's natural hot springs are a unique experience that offers visitors the opportunity to relax in a spectacular natural setting and enjoy the benefits of the thermal waters. Choosing to visit Costa Rica's sustainable natural hot springs also means supporting the local environment and the country's sustainable economy.

CHAPTER 4

WHAT TO EAT IN COST RICA?

Typical dishes from the local cuisine of Costa Rica

Costa Rican cuisine is rich in fresh, spicy flavors, with dishes that are a fusion of Spanish, African, and indigenous influences. Flavors are generally simple but strong, and dishes often contain rice, beans, meat, fish, and vegetables. Here are some of the typical dishes of Costa Rica's local cuisine:

Gallo Pinto: Costa Rica's national dish, Gallo Pinto, is a combination of rice and black beans with onions, cilantro, and spices. It is often served for breakfast with eggs, cheese and tortillas.

Casado: this dish is a complete, traditional meal that includes rice and beans, meat or fish, vegetables such as cabbage or lettuce, fried plantain, and a typical sauce called Lizano.

Arroz con Pollo: A delicious combination of rice and chicken cooked with vegetables such as carrots, peas and peppers. This dish is often served with fresh avocado and a cilantro sauce.

Olla de Carne: a rich and hearty soup with beef, potatoes, carrots, yucca and other vegetables. It is often served with rice and beans.

Cevice: a dish of raw fish marinated in lime, cilantro and other ingredients, it is often served with tortillas or crackers.

Tamales: a traditional holiday dish in Costa Rica, they are made of corn stuffed with meat, rice, vegetables and spices. They are wrapped in banana leaves and steamed.

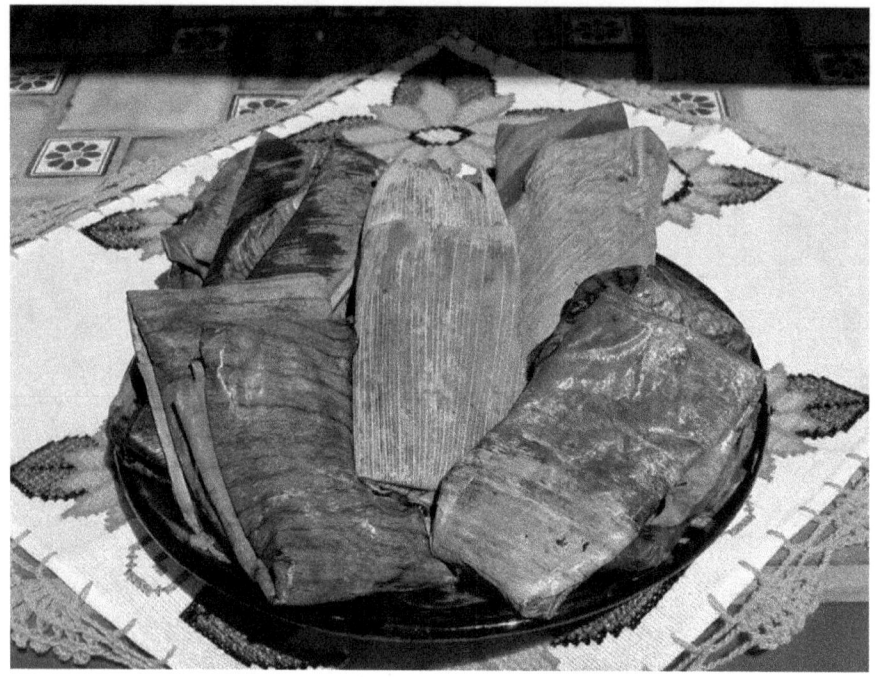

Platano maduro: a dish made from ripe plantains sliced and fried in oil, often served as a side dish or snack.

Chifrijo: a popular bar dish consisting of rice, black beans, pork and avocado, served with corn chips.

Tamal de Elote: similar to tamale, but made with fresh corn instead of cornmeal. It is often filled with chicken or pork and served with a spicy sauce.

Sopa Negra: a black bean soup served with hard-boiled eggs, rice, garlic, and onions.

Costa Rica's cuisine is a real treat for adventurous palates, offering a variety of flavorful and spicy dishes that are a must for any visitor to the country.

Traditional drinks such as coffee and guaro from the Costa Rica

Costa Rica is known for its high-quality coffee production, with a long history in coffee cultivation and processing. Costa Rican coffee is appreciated worldwide for its robust and intense flavor, with notes of fruit and chocolate. In Costa Rica, most coffee plantations are located in the country's central mountainous regions, such as the Valle Central.

In Costa Rica, coffee is a very important beverage and is consumed in the traditional way using the filtration method known as chorreador. The coffee is poured slowly through a cloth filter placed on a carafe, creating a smooth and aromatic drink. Costa Rican coffee is often accompanied by a local sweet or cookie, such as bizcocho or chorreada.

Another traditional Costa Rican drink is guaro, a sugarcane distillate that is popular throughout the country. Guaro is a clear white liquor with a slightly sweet taste and a high alcohol content, usually around 35-40%. It is often served as a base for cocktails or drunk neat in small glasses.

In addition to coffee and guaro, Costa Rica also produces a variety of fresh fruit juices, such as pineapple, mango, guava, and maracuja juice. These juices are often served in restaurants and local markets and are a delicious alternative to classic alcoholic drinks.

Finally, Costa Rica's local beer is Imperial, a light and refreshing beer that is widely available throughout the country. It is often served cold with a piece of lemon and pairs perfectly with local dishes, such as ceviche or gallo pinto.

20 Most Important Restaurants in Costa Rica

Here is a brief description of each recommended restaurant:

Restaurante Grano de Oro - San Jose: Elegant restaurant serving Costa Rican and international dishes with a great selection of wines.

Restaurante Silvestre - San Jose: Gourmet restaurant serving creative dishes inspired by local cuisine.

Restaurante El Patio del Balmoral - San Jose: Cozy and casual restaurant serving Costa Rican and international dishes.

Tin Jo - San Jose: Asian cuisine restaurant with a wide selection of sushi, noodles and grilled dishes.

Restaurante Casa Rolandi - San Jose: Mexican restaurant with a wide selection of traditional dishes, from tacos to fajitas.

Restaurante Kaixo - San Jose: Basque cuisine restaurant with a selection of meat and fish dishes.

Restaurante Naans & Curries - San Jose: Indian restaurant serving curries and tandoori dishes.

Soda y Marisquería Siete Mares - Puntarenas: Beachfront restaurant specializing in fresh fish and seafood dishes.

Restaurante El Avion - Manuel Antonio: Restaurant with stunning ocean views and a military plane converted into a bar.

Falafel Bar - Manuel Antonio: Vegetarian restaurant serving falafel, hummus and other Middle Eastern dishes.

Emilio's Cafe - Dominical: International cuisine restaurant with a wide selection of meat and fish dishes.

Restaurante Claro Que Si - Arenal: Costa Rican cuisine restaurant with a wide selection of meat and fish dishes.

Restaurante Lava Lounge - Arenal: Beachfront restaurant serving fresh fish and seafood dishes.

Lizard King Resort - Tamarindo: Restaurant with a great selection of meat and seafood dishes, including their famous tuna filet.

El Coconut Beach Club - Tamarindo: Beachfront restaurant specializing in fresh fish and seafood dishes.

Soda La Parada - Monteverde: Costa Rican cuisine restaurant serving traditional dishes such as gallo pinto.

Restaurante El Jardin - Monteverde: Restaurant with a great selection of meat and seafood dishes, including their famous grilled chicken.

Soda El Tucán - Puerto Viejo de Talamanca: Beachside restaurant serving fresh fish and seafood dishes.

Restaurante Bread and Chocolate - Puerto Viejo de Talamanca: Vegetarian restaurant specializing in sandwiches, salads and homemade desserts.

Soda Mar y Tierra - Limon: Costa Rican cuisine restaurant with a wide selection of meat and seafood dishes.

CHAPTER 5

PRATICAL TIPS FOR TRAVELING IN COSTA RICA

For most tourists, a visa is not required to enter Costa Rica, but you must have a passport valid for at least six months from the date of arrival. Italian citizens can stay in the country for up to 90 days without a visa.

Upon arrival, tourists will be asked to provide proof of departure, such as a return ticket or a ticket to another country. Alternatively, tourists can provide a certificate of asylum application or a certificate of residence permit.

In addition, it is advisable to bring a copy of your passport, as well as a copy of your health insurance. It is important to keep in mind that many tour operators and accommodations require their clients to sign a document confirming that they are aware of the country's rules regarding ecotourism and respect for the environment.

It is also important to keep in mind that special permits may be required to visit some nature reserves or protected areas. However, these permits can usually be obtained easily at the access point of the reserve or protected area.

Finally, you should contact the Costa Rican embassy or consulate in your country to see if there are any additional requirements or documents needed for your stay in the country.

U.S. citizens do not need a visa to enter Costa Rica as tourists for stays of up to 90 days. However, tourists will be required to provide a passport valid for at least six months from the date of arrival, as well as proof of departure, such as a return ticket or ticket to another country.

In addition, all travelers entering Costa Rica from abroad are required to complete an online health form, known as the "Pase de Salud," which requires them to provide certain health information, travel itinerary, and intended accommodation. Once the form is completed, a QR code will be provided that must be presented upon arrival in Costa Rica.

You should also always check with the Costa Rican embassy or consulate in the United States if there are any additional requirements or documents needed for your stay in the country.

Costa Rica is generally a safe country for tourists, but as in any other country, there are some precautions you should take to ensure your personal safety and health.

First of all, it is advisable to avoid carrying unnecessary valuables while traveling and to always maintain special vigilance in popular tourist areas, such as beaches or pedestrian zones. Also, it is advisable not to leave valuables unattended in the hotel room or car.

It is also advisable not to walk alone or at night in less frequented or dimly lit areas. It is advisable to always ask qualified personnel for information, such as hotel reception or national park rangers.

Regarding health, Costa Rica is a relatively safe destination from a health standpoint, but it is always best to take precautions to avoid illness. In particular, it is important to drink potable or bottled water and use only ice that has been prepared with potable or bottled water. Also, it is advisable to always wash fruits and vegetables before eating them.

Regarding mosquito-borne diseases, such as Zika virus, dengue and malaria, it is advisable to use insect repellent containing DEET and wear protective clothing, such as long pants and long-sleeved shirts.

Finally, it is advisable to carry a personal first aid kit, containing medication for headaches, indigestion and other common symptoms, as well as customized medical supplies, such as eyeglasses for those who need them.

It is also advisable to consult with your doctor or a local immunization center before leaving for Costa Rica to see if you need specific vaccines for your health.

In Costa Rica, the main means of transportation for tourists are the bus, cab, rental car, and airplanes.

The bus is the cheapest means of transportation and the most used by Costa Ricans. The main bus company is the "Empresa de Transporte Público" (ETP), which offers regular and reliable services throughout the country. Buses are generally clean and well-maintained, but they can get very crowded during peak hours.

Cabs are another common transportation option in Costa Rica. Official cabs can be recognized by their orange-red color, but there are also many private cabs operating in the area. It is recommended to use only official cabs and to agree on the price before leaving.

Car rental is a popular option for tourists who wish to explore the country independently. The main car rental companies operating in Costa Rica include Avis, Budget, Hertz, National and Thrifty. It is advisable to book in advance, as car rentals can be in high demand during peak seasons.

For longer trips, airplanes are a convenient and fast option. Major airlines operating in Costa Rica include Avianca, Copa Airlines, Delta Air Lines, Southwest Airlines, and United Airlines. Costa Rica's national airline is "Nature Air," which offers domestic flights at affordable fares.

In addition, there is also an extensive network of private shuttle services connecting the country's major cities and tourist attractions. These shuttle services are often very affordable and reliable and can be booked in advance through local tour operators or directly from the transportation companies.

In Costa Rica, there are many types of accommodations to choose from, from luxurious resorts to simple guesthouses. Here are some suggestions for lodging based on different budget needs:

Hostels: there are many hostels throughout Costa Rica, especially in the larger cities and tourist areas. This is an affordable option for low-budget travelers. Prices vary depending on location and facilities offered, but generally hostel dorms cost about $10 to $20 per night.

Vacation homes: if you are traveling in a group or family, renting a vacation home can be an affordable option. There are many short-term vacation rentals in Costa Rica, offering amenities such as kitchen, living room and outdoor spaces. Prices vary depending on the location and size of the house, but generally start from about $50-100 per night.

Bed & Breakfast: there are many guesthouses and Bed & Breakfasts in Costa Rica, which offer a more personal lodging experience. These facilities can be more expensive than hostels, but often offer breakfast included. Prices vary depending on location and facilities offered, but generally start at about $50-100 per night.

Hotels: there are many hotels in Costa Rica, ranging from luxurious resorts to budget hotels. The price varies depending on the location, size of the hotel, and facilities offered. Generally, a budget hotel can cost around $50-100 per night, while a luxurious resort can cost over $200 per night.

In general, Costa Rica is a relatively expensive country in terms of lodging, especially in tourist areas. However, there are still ways to save money, such as booking in advance, looking for special offers, and considering lodging options outside the tourist areas.

Also, to save money on food, it is advisable to choose accommodations with kitchens and prepare your own meals. This way, you can buy fresh local produce and save on restaurant costs.

Here is a list of 15 luxury resorts in Costa Rica with a brief description of each:

Four Seasons Resort Costa Rica at Peninsula Papagayo: Located on the northwest coast of Costa Rica, this resort offers luxury accommodations and an 18-hole golf course.

Andaz Costa Rica Resort at Peninsula Papagayo: This boutique resort is also located at Peninsula Papagayo and is surrounded by lush rainforest. It offers a wide range of outdoor activities.

Nayara Springs: This resort is nestled in the jungle near Arenal Volcano National Park and offers a luxury experience with great attention to detail.

Villa Buena Onda: Located on the Pacific coast of Costa Rica, this adults-only boutique resort offers luxury and relaxation in a tranquil atmosphere.

El Mangroove, Autograph Collection: This resort is located in the rainforest near the Liberia airport and offers spectacular views of the Gulf of Papagayo.

Hotel Punta Islita, Autograph Collection: This boutique resort is located on the Pacific coast of Costa Rica and is surrounded by beautiful rainforest.

Secrets Papagayo Costa Rica: This adults-only resort is located on the Pacific coast and offers luxury accommodations, gourmet restaurants, and an array of outdoor activities.

Hotel Capitan Suizo: This boutique hotel is located on the beach in Tamarindo and offers a luxury experience in a tropical setting.

The Westin Golf Resort & Spa, Playa Conchal: Located on the Pacific coast, this resort offers an 18-hole golf course and a variety of outdoor activities.

Los Suenos Marriott Ocean & Golf Resort: This resort is located on the Pacific coast and offers an 18-hole golf course, a luxury spa, and spectacular ocean views.

W Costa Rica - Reserva Conchal: This resort is located on the Pacific coast and offers a modern luxury experience in a natural setting.

Hotel Punta Leona: Located on the Pacific coast, this resort offers luxury accommodations and access to a private beach.

Hotel Costa Verde: This resort is located near Manuel Antonio National Park and offers luxury accommodations with views of the rainforest.

Dreams Las Mareas Costa Rica: This resort is located on the Pacific coast and offers a wide range of outdoor activities and gourmet restaurants.

JW Marriott Guanacaste Resort & Spa: Located on the Pacific coast, this resort offers an 18-hole golf course and a luxury spa.

CHAPTER 6

OTHER TIPS TO TRAVELING IN COSTA RICA

Choosing places to visit in Costa Rica depends on each traveler's personal preferences and interests. However, there are some destinations that are considered must-sees:

- Corcovado National Park, with its unique fauna and flora;
- The Nicoya Peninsula, for its breathtaking beaches and

relaxed atmosphere;
- Arenal Volcano, for its hot springs and outdoor activities;
- Tortuguero National Park, for its natural beauty and sea turtle watching;
- The city of Puerto Viejo, on the Caribbean coast, for its Afro-Caribbean culture and black sand beaches.

In addition, for those who are fond of outdoor activities, Costa Rica offers many options, such as rafting on river rapids, hiking in rainforests, surfing on Pacific and Caribbean Sea beaches, snorkeling and deep-sea fishing.

Finally, for those who love food, Costa Rica offers a unique and flavorful cuisine, with dishes of rice, beans, meat, and fresh fish, accompanied by local spices such as cilantro and chili peppers. In addition, you cannot miss tasting the local coffee and sugarcane rum, two of the country's traditional drinks.

Overall, Costa Rica is an ideal destination for those seeking a combination of nature, adventure, culture, and relaxation. There are many options for all tastes and budgets, and the kindness and hospitality of Costa Ricans will surely make the trip even more memorable.

Corcovado National Park: Located on the Pacific coast, Corcovado National Park is considered one of the most beautiful and wild parks in the world. Many species of animals such as jaguars, pumas, tapirs, monkeys and many tropical birds can be found here. There are also many breathtaking beaches, such as Playa de Sirena, where whales can be seen during migration season.

Nicoya Peninsula: Located on the Pacific coast, the Nicoya Peninsula is famous for its white sandy beaches, crystal clear waters and relaxed atmosphere. There are many coastal towns and villages that offer a wide range of outdoor activities such as surfing, snorkeling, fishing, and hiking. In addition, it is a great place to observe wildlife such as primates and tropical birds.

Arenal Volcano: Located in the northwestern region of the country, Arenal Volcano is one of the most active volcanoes in the world. The natural hot springs nearby are perfect for relaxing after a day of outdoor activities, such as trekking, horseback riding and rafting on river rapids. In addition, there are many opportunities to observe wildlife in the area, such as cougars and crocodiles.

Tortuguero National Park: Located on the Caribbean coast, Tortuguero National Park is a vast area of mangroves, canals and lagoons. It is famous for its natural beauty and its population of sea turtles. During spawning season, green turtles and giant tortoises can be seen arriving on the beach to lay their eggs. There are also numerous outdoor activities such as kayaking in the canals, hiking in the rainforests, and wildlife watching.

The city of Puerto Viejo: Located on the Caribbean coast, the city of Puerto Viejo is famous for its Afro-Caribbean culture, relaxed atmosphere, and black sand beaches. Here you can find numerous restaurants and bars offering traditional food and drinks, such as chicken curry and local rum. In addition, there are many outdoor activities such as surfing, snorkeling, and wildlife watching.

Overall, these places offer a wide range of outdoor activities, beautiful beaches, and abundant wildlife and are considered some of Costa Rica's top tourist attractions.

Fun Fucts about Costa Rica

Costa Rica, we have been writing for some time, is in many ways a special country. I tried to imagine some characteristics that best distinguish it and came up with this list, not exhaustive but certainly significant.

pura vida "Pura Vida" is not just an 'expression: it is a philosophy of life.

You will hear this expression all the time from Costa Ricans, or if you prefer from Ticos as they use to call themselves. Beyond the literal meaning, the phrase is used as a greeting or to say "thank you" or "you're welcome" or that "everything is fine." It is also not infrequently used to emphasize the need to accept and relieve some situation in life. But "pura vida" is also a philosophy that needs to be understood because it means knowing how to grasp the simple things in life, freeing oneself from unnecessary stress and living in harmony with nature. Could it be why Costa Rica almost always ranks high in the rankings of the happiest countries in the world ? In any case, it is an 'art that we recommend practicing.

autoAddresses are not necessary here.

Almost everywhere in Costa Rica there are no street names or house numbers. Ticos are used to giving directions with cardinal points and distances in meters from a known point. You might therefore hear directions such as, "50 meters North and 150 meters West from the Church of Santa Teresita" . In some cases in urban areas you might hear about the "cuadra" which refers to the block; but be careful because here a block is always worth 100 meters on the side even though it may measure much less or more. And if the reference point no longer exists the Tico is not discouraged at all because he will tell you for example : ".... 100 meters from the ancient mango tree ". It sounds crazy but it usually works

Here it is impossible to find a crowded beach.

With 1200 km of coastline on two oceans Costa Rica has an incredible amount of beautiful beaches. Beaches truly for all tastes: romantic and secluded, trendy for sipping an aperitif with friends, for taking a sunset ride, for snorkeling and fishing... And really very rarely will you find one crowded except during the Christmas (La Navidad) and Easter (La Semana Santa) holidays in which it is recommended to stay strictly away from them because all the Ticos flock there en masse armed with tents, coolers, speakers and much more that often harms the tranquility of others. At all other times of the year, however, it is not unlikely to find large stretches of beach exclusively for you.

Monkeys are very talented thieves.

While hiking in Costa Rica's national parks, particularly in Manuel Antonio on the Pacific side and Cahuita on the Caribbean side, be very careful of certain cunning thieves. Delightful, small, hairy and prehensile-tailed Cariblanco or Cappuccina monkeys, two of the four species of monkeys native to Costa Rica, are known for their ability to open backpacks left unattended by unsuspecting tourists. Once they have their prey chasing them is completely useless, they will disappear into the branches scattering what you have in the forest and holding food for themselves, if any are found

Casa do Rice and beans every day ? try it !

Start your day with "Gallo Pinto" the typical breakfast dish of well-mixed beans and rice, onion, chili and culantro served with scrambled or fried eggs, cream cheese and the ubiquitous "Lizano sauce." At lunch reach for your favorite soda and order a "casado" true national dish of rice, black beans, salad and ripe plantain accompanied by meat, chicken or fish. Interesting is the Caribbean version called "rice and beans" sweetened by coconut milk that is added to the cooking water. And for an evening snack try (if you can) a chifrijo, rice and beans topped with chicharrones (fried pork chunks), accompanied by "pico de gallo" (chopped tomato, cilantro and onion with lime juice) or a guacamole (avocado, onions tomato and chili) served with fried corn chips

coffeeA sock is what you need to make a wonderful coffee.

A newcomer to Costa Rica might visit a local kitchen and wonder with some amazement what a sock hanging on a small wooden hoop is for. Well, that sock is nothing more than an ingenious and inexpensive filter for making good "chorreado" coffee, which is made by simply putting the right amount of coffee inside it and slowly running very hot water through it. The "chorreador" allows you to prepare an excellent "Cafecito", A very different drink from our espresso coffee but, believe me, the aroma of good coffee prepared in that way is irresistible.

playa Naranjo Only two seasons ! So many seasons

Costa Rica, on the central Pacific side, the most visited side of the country, technically has only two seasons: the Verano, or 'summer, which is the dry season and runs from December to April, and the invierno which is the rainy season, also called the "green" season, which runs from May to November. During the dry season most of the country receives little or no rain, and in the rainy season these are generally limited to afternoons and nights. It is important to note, however, that the Caribbean side of Costa Rica follows different weather patterns and that it can rain at any time of year . Not to mention that there are at least ten other different climate zones in the country. All this is to say: that whatever weather pattern you prefer, and whatever activity you want to be engaged in, there is never a wrong time to travel to Costa Rica.

mercado san joseThe weather in Costa Rica is "Tempo Tico."

Costa Ricans call it " la hora tica," and it is a decidedly more relaxed way of thinking about time than normal time. "We have dinner at eight o'clock," for example, could be interpreted as " dinner will be at eight thirty or even nine o'clock." Tempo Tico, is part of what makes Costa Rica as a place where it is easy to escape from the rigid structure that governs the daily life and time of so many of us. This phenomenon is also well understood in the language The word ahora, which means " now" in Spanish, here means instead " later" or " at some unspecified time in the future." So if you are told " ahora lo hago" it means nothing more than " I will do it later" or " I will do it in a while." But certainly not now. Given the innate kindness of the Ticos you might at best hear them say, " ahorita " which sweetens a pill that for us can be rather bitter but, believe me, absolutely unavoidable.

Chiguirro Listening to a bird is the best way to predict the weather.

Every year at a stroke, at the end of Costa Rica's summer, the yigüirro a lovely clay-colored bird sings to anticipate the beginning of the rainy season. You will no doubt hear it in its high voice just before dawn, when you are still asleep. In a country known for its flamboyant avian species, it is he, anonymous in his inconspicuous livery, who has been chosen as Costa Rica's national bird for his melodious song heralding the impending rains.

San Jose is the capital of Costa Rica and the cultural, political and economic center of the country. Founded in 1738, it was originally called "Villa Nueva de la Boca del Monte" and later renamed "San Jose" in honor of St. Joseph.

CHAPTER 7

SAN JOSE

The city of San Jose is located in the central valley of the country, surrounded by mountains and volcanoes. Its geographical location makes it an ideal destination for exploring the entire country, as it is located in the center of the main roads leading to the Pacific and Atlantic beaches, mountains, and nature reserves in the area.

The city of San Jose is divided into several neighborhoods, each with its own characteristics. The historic center, known as "El Centro," is the beating heart of the city and is where the main tourist attractions, restaurants and stores are located. Walking through its streets, you can admire Spanish colonial architecture with colorful buildings, wrought-iron balconies and tree-lined squares.

Among the main attractions in the historic center are the Metropolitan Cathedral, the National Theater, the Central Market, and the National Museum. The Metropolitan Cathedral, located on the Plaza de la Cultura, is an imposing neoclassical building built in 1871. The National Theater, also located on the Plaza de la Cultura, is a magnificent neoclassical-style building built in 1897. The Central Market is a must-see for food lovers, with its many stalls selling fruits, vegetables, meat, fish, and local dishes such as gallo pinto. The National Museum is housed in an old neoclassical building and features an extensive collection of pre-Columbian objects, including ceramics, sculptures and jewelry.

The Barrio Amon district, located north of the historic center, is famous for its Victorian architecture and art nouveau buildings. Numerous restaurants, bars, and fashion boutiques can be found here. The Escalante neighborhood, east of the historic center, has become the hangout for young people and hipsters and is known for its trendy restaurants and bars.

The San Pedro district, located south of the historic center, is the city's university area and is bustling with nightlife. Numerous restaurants, bars and clubs can be found here. The Rohrmoser district, located west of the historic center, is one of the city's most residential neighborhoods and is known for its large villas and parks.

San Jose is also famous for its museums, including the Museum of Pre-Columbian Gold, the Museum of Costa Rican Art, and the Museum of Contemporary Art and Design. The Museum of Precolumbian Gold.

COSTA RICA TRAVEL GUIDE 2023

The National Theater is the flagship of San José. Its most iconic building, because of what it represents, but also because of its architectural details. That's why you'll find it on many advertising posters, postcards, and magnets. It is located in the center of the capital, a classical style was used, and it was finished in 1897. A coffee tax was even introduced to support its construction. Guided tours inside the rooms can be arranged in English and Spanish.

Pre-Columbian Gold Museum

Here you will admire more than 1,500 gold objects belonging to the pre-Columbian peoples who lived in present-day Costa Rican territory. It is a very rich museum that explains the importance of the objects in the daily life of different civilizations. All the items in the collection date from between 500 and 1500, in a journey through jewelry, artifacts, historical coins, but also representations of regional art. The museum, located under the Plaza de la Cultura, is owned by Banco Central and its architecture is reminiscent of a bank vault.

Museo del Jade
Another curious visit to make in San Jose is to the Jade Museum.

The building has a large collection of pottery, gold, and other materials, but its main attraction is the world's largest collection of jade objects. The museum has five permanent thematic exhibition halls, where Costa Rica's ancient history is told through an archaeological interpretation that highlights the social, religious, and everyday aspects of the people who made and used the objects on display.

National Museum

This is one of the most interesting museums, starting with its location, an old historic barracks, declared a historical architectural heritage site and a symbol of the abolition of the army in Costa Rica. Its exhibition halls show the various collections in the areas of national history, archaeology, and natural history. It hosts temporary exhibitions on artistic and cultural themes and offers a varied agenda of activities throughout the year.

Central Marketplace

Visiting the Central Market is another of the things to do in San Jose. Open since 1880, it has been declared a Cultural Heritage Site for its distinctive features and historical identity. Its narrow alleys are home to more than 200 stores, stalls and restaurants. Without a doubt, a good place to get acquainted with the local atmosphere. The market is very distinctive for meat, while on the stalls you can taste papaya, "chayote," lychee, or cas (a sweet and sour fruit used as a base for fresca, a sour fruit drink). You can also buy a wide variety of exotic products such as flowers, herbs and medicines.

La Sabana Park

At 72 hectares, this park is the largest public space in San Jose and the most visited in the country. It is very common to see ticos (the nickname for Costa Ricans) playing sports, playing ball, or just walking around. Although it may not look like it, the park is located 1,100 meters above sea level. Most residents unplug a bit from the city chaos in this green lung.

Costa Rican Art Museum

The Museo de Arte Costarricense (MAC) coordinates the main activities related to the visual arts in Costa Rica: it collects and exhibits works by national and international artists, and stimulates artistic discussion and critical thinking also through educational and recreational programs. The MAC has more than six thousand works in its collection that includes painting, sculpture, photography, and other works by national and international artists, spanning a historical period from the mid-1800s to the early 21st century.

Culture Square

San Jose

This square is one of the best known and busiest in San Jose. Partly because it is right in the center of the capital, and then it is a fine setting that houses the Jade Museum, the National Theater, and the Museum of Pre-Columbian Gold. The Plaza de la Cultura was built in 1973, shortly after the National Theater was recognized as a monument of historical interest. It is a particularly busy place where street life with clowns, jugglers, street vendors, and performers can be seen.

National Stadium

The National Stadium is located in the La Sabana Metropolitan Park, and was completed in 2011, opening its doors the same year.It has a capacity of more than 35 thousand spectators and is a multipurpose facility that also hosts events, concerts, and sporting events. It is the home of the Costa Rican national soccer team.

Take a cruise to the Caribbean

The Caribbean will give you many corners of absolute enchantment where nature will be the protagonist, along with the colors of an endless summer and the good humor of the inhabitants. Lots of sunshine, things to do and many reasons to get excited and have unforgettable memories to share await you. Sea, curiosities and many stops to appreciate with our excursions. Costa Rica is then one of the places where the inhabitants are the happiest in the world, so why not take advantage of it?

COSTA RICA TRAVEL GUIDE 2023

CHAPTER 8

MONTE VERDE

Monteverde is a tourist resort located in the mountains of Costa Rica, famous for its biodiversity and natural scenic beauty.

One of Monteverde's main attractions is the Bosque Nuboso Monteverde Biological Reserve, a protected area covering about 10,500 hectares of montane and cloud forest. The reserve is famous for its wide variety of fauna and flora, including more than 2,500 species of plants, 100 species of mammals, 400 species of birds, and thousands of insects. Among the reserve's most popular hiking trails are Sendero Bosque Nuboso and Sendero El Camino.

Another popular attraction in Monteverde is Bosque Eterno de los Niños, a nature reserve managed by children from Costa Rica and around the world. The reserve covers an area of 22,500 hectares and is the result of a fundraising campaign launched in the 1980s by children around the world to save the Monteverde mountain rainforest.

COSTA RICA TRAVEL GUIDE 2023

In terms of restaurants, Monteverde offers a wide range of dining options. Popular restaurants include the Tree House Restaurant, located in a tree house 20 feet above the ground, Restaurante Amigos, which serves traditional Costa Rican dishes such as casado, and Sofia Mediterranean Cuisine, which specializes in Mediterranean cuisine.

In general, Monteverde is a very attractive tourist destination for nature and adventure lovers, with numerous activities such as hiking or horseback riding, tree walks, zip-lines, and more.

There are numerous lodging options in Monteverde for every taste and budget, including hotels, resorts, hostels, bed & breakfasts, and vacation rentals. Here are some notable resorts:

Hotel Belmar: an eco-friendly resort located in the Monteverde rainforest, with comfortable rooms and breathtaking views of the valley. The hotel also has an organic restaurant serving local and international dishes.

El Establo Mountain Hotel & Private Reserve: a 4-star resort with spacious and luxurious rooms, many with views of the Gulf of Nicoya. The resort also has an indoor pool, tennis court, spa, and gourmet restaurant.

Monteverde Lodge & Gardens: an eco-friendly resort with comfortable and spacious rooms set in a tropical garden. The resort also has a restaurant serving fresh, local dishes.

Senda Monteverde Hotel: a 4-star resort located in the Monteverde Rainforest with spacious, modern rooms and panoramic views of the valley. The resort also has an outdoor pool, a gourmet restaurant, and a spa.

Hotel Fonda Vela: a resort located on a hill overlooking the Monteverde forest, with spacious and comfortable rooms. The resort also has an outdoor pool, a restaurant serving international dishes, and a bar.

In addition to these resorts, there are many other accommodation options in Monteverde that can meet the needs of any traveler.

COSTA RICA TRAVEL GUIDE 2023

Printed in the USA
CPSIA information can be obtained
at www.ICGtesting.com
LVHW011638270923
759522LV00044B/800